THE APPLE BARREL

Jon Stallworthy

THE APPLE BARREL

Selected Poems
1955-63

London
OXFORD UNIVERSITY PRESS
NEW YORK TORONTO
1974

Oxford University Press, Ely House, London W.1
GLASGOW NEW YORK TORONTO MELBOURNE WELLINGTON
CAPE TOWN IBADAN NAIROBI DAR ES SALAAM LUSAKA ADDIS ABABA
DELHI BOMBAY CALCUTTA MADRAS KARACHI LAHORE DACCA
KUALA LUMPUR SINGAPORE HONG KONG TOKYO

ISBN 0 19 211837 4

Printed in Great Britain by
The Bowering Press Limited
Plymouth

For Jill

Prefatory Note

Virginia Woolf advised a young poet not to publish before he was thirty. I had not heard this when, at the age of twenty-five, I came to assemble my first book of poems and even if I had, would probably have disregarded it.

Thirteen years later, I see the wisdom in her advice: poets of twenty-five can seldom distinguish between their good poems and their flawed ones, and I put too many of the latter into *The Astronomy of Love* and into its sequel, *Out of Bounds*. Some of the better poems have continued to find their way into anthologies, although both books have been out of print for a number of years.

I am grateful to those who bought them and to those who still ask for them for giving me this opportunity to throw out the rotten poems and make a second choice of those that seem worth their place in the apple barrel.

Contents

A Lesson in Astronomy

THE astronomy of love is this :
by night, when heaven glows
pale between your arms, to kiss
a constellation of ten toes.

Then kiss the glimmering knees that point
to larger planets in love's chart,
and through the hips' wide orbit mount
the milky way towards her heart.

Kiss the pole-star navel next
like a god in your ascent.
Pause, but do not be perplexed
by twin moons in the firmament.

Kiss the seven stars in her face;
and in her ultimate dark hair
touch infinity, or retrace
your journey on the glittering stair.

Love's astronomy is to watch
where one starred body lies;
always to see, but never touch,
that body in the naked skies.

The Common Breath

THE amber body and the white
sustained one tumult through that night,
struggling each in dumb distress
to slough their passionate loneliness.
Their hands would strip the spirit bare
and toss the flesh across a chair.
They breathe together : under the heat
urged by the bellows, under the beat
of pulses hammering, they would forge
one self in armour. But the large
lance of the sun shall run them through.
They shall wake not one, but two;
mocked, while alternate hammers fall,
by the one shadow on the wall.
Dully at morning, when the rain
knuckles the nervous window pane,
they dress : and in that hour she loathes
the body crumpled as her clothes.
He ties his smile, but underneath
the whistle's broken in his teeth.

The amber body and the white
lie in separate beds tonight.
Double bolster, space and time
keep them so : for she will climb
to moon-drift linen, when the man
watches day open like a fan
against another sky. No gulf
driven between self and self
by the estranging ocean, may
more distance them than when they lay
knocking side by knocking side,

satiate but unsatisfied.
Tomorrow, if the small, hard rain
carry him to her bed again
he will join his hands behind his head,
perplexed, to think that if he read
in some black column of her death,
he loses of their common breath
only so much as would suppress
his whistling for a day; or less.

La Ronde

CARELESS on their isle of time
how the nighted oceans rave,
lovers lying lip on lip
live the love they cannot save.

Live the love they cannot, save
for that night: there lives but this—
heartache for a chalice spilt
from the fury of their kiss.

From the fury of their kiss
turning when the lust shall fail,
lovers murmur as they sleep:
'What goes under in the gale?'

What goes under in the gale,
when their isle's foundations shift,
each will learn, who wakes alone
on the rafted soul adrift.

On the rafted soul adrift
certain I, while oceans rave,
lovers lying lip on lip
live the love I could not save.

Song at the Turning of the Tide

O DO not let the levelling sea,
the rub and scrub of the wave,
scour me out or cover me
with sand in a shallow grave.

But let my image, like a rock
contemptuous of the tide's attack,
shift no inch at the green shock
and glisten when the wave springs back.

A Reminder

A SILVER chain, too small
for crucifix or charms,
on work-days she would wear,
not for conceit, but all
because my arms
could not be fastened there.

The one pearl in the chain
she, with her finger-tips,
would touch as if aware
of loss perhaps, or pain
because my lips
could not be fastened there.

In even the wind's throat
breath runs out, and time becalms
not only sailing ships.
Remind her, chain and pearl,
how I who loved her wrote
that, grown old, she should wear
this relic of the girl;
because my arms,
because my lips
were sometime fastened there.

Romance

WHY, when my head was filled
with maidens for whose sake
kings sold their castles, headsmen felled
a forest of tall princes, and
the woodcutter's sons were drowned in the lake;

why, when my heroines
sang Te Deums from the rack;
from faggots rampant at their shins;
or, tossed between sea and sand,
elbowed the lighthouse dinghy to the wreck;

why should I look, not once,
but ever since, answer me that,
at you with no falcon nor lance
but a basket in your hand,
and, for a crown, your least heraldic hat?

You not with Me

WALKING—but you not with me—round
a glass sky fallen into Blenheim lake,
I see the wind's invisible dancers waltz
from hill to water, and the cloud-floes break
superbly into swans. And I
who know what songs the fields are singing, drowned
in their green wave, know that the singers lie.
The rooks trumpet for summer on a false
alarm. Else why should you, my swan,
be restless to move on?

Our inward weather does not take
its season from the year. Below that beech
once in a roaring month we could not see
leaves dancing like the damned, nor heard them preach
warning of winter. All that day
the skeletons wore green again, the lake
stole colour from your eyes. Long as you lay
between my arms, the wide arms of the tree
would let no leaf, or squall, or wing
intrude upon our spring.

So long as April weather filled
the heart, we lived the poems of our love
without restraint of intellect or rhyme.
Just to perfect the living was enough,
when all along the avenue
and in the hedge we saw the small birds build :
and though no bird in all that summer flew
nearer to heaven's lake, when had we time
in the astonishment of spring
to stretch the throat and sing?

The ancient serpent, tooth in tail,
now stirring at the centre of the world
turns also in the heart. A season ends,
and love's tranquillity at last is thrown
into the violent ditch. I see
our reason bending to the body's gale
and stripped as naked as the beaten tree.
Naked I am : but safe from crossing winds
of love, my white bird disappears
against a squall of tears.

May you in this migration find
summer beneath your wings, as when we brushed
a winter's slate sky clean. Till you return
no spring can rustle in the blood, now hushed
and frozen with a final kiss.
Over the desolate waters of the mind
the storm advances. Gathered into this
upon the dark lake's darkest edge, I learn
it is the breaking of the wing
teaches the swan to sing.

Boy and Fox

LITTLE fox, little fox, with your brush of hair,
I have carried you everywhere
all day against my skin. I said
no calloused hand shall rub the head
I fondle, nor shall curious eyes
explore your body like gross flies.
Jump up, and you shall keep me warm.
How could I guess that you would worm
your muzzle through my ribs, and tear
tissue from bone as if your lair
lay in my stomach? From the wound
my heart bangs like a sail in the wind
about to split with its own thunder.
Split heart, and spill your thunder.
Little fox, work on, and gnaw
every root to the red core
until, drum-bellied, you lie down
curled in a cavity of bone.
Then let us sleep and think we know
a kinder consummation. Now
from the Spartan I would learn
to joke and whistle in the lane
louder than the nagging teeth:
but how shall I conceal beneath
the white stare of this face, this shirt,
the creeping colour of my hurt?

What every Wise Man's Son doth Know

BALBOA, when the mountains split
before a wedge of silver, must have cursed
the pikemen who could only spit;
and captains ignorant of a lifetime's thirst
who snatched the cup of silence from his lips.
Whose finger stabbed, who shouted first,
no one remembered when they reached their ships.

Others trudge lonely from the beach,
carrying silence with them like a stone
through swamp and jungle; till a leech
of terror fastens onto every bone.
All who cross lonely over pass and ford
cross twice for being alone;
but when the mountains break have their reward.

Last night a ridge of linen snow
quilted my feet, and four months misery
slid from my back. There arched below
such a pacific and astounding sea,
such islands, inlets, and white-sanded shores,
I found that one man's love can be
more than the triumph of conquistadors.

The Master-Mariner's Epithalamion

THERE was a captain who, weary of land,
called for his swallow-tail coat and cravat,
his buckle-shoes, spyglass, and tricorne hat;
and called on deck a thumping band
to stuff the sails. From bollard, quay,
and painted hulls,
a squall of gulls
blew him over the switchback sea.

Twelve days out in the roaring lanes
a mutinous crew beat down his door.
Some he pistolled on the cabin floor,
marlin-spiked the bosun's brains
and clapped the deck-hands into irons;
but at his back
on every tack
pounced the sea like a pride of lions.

There was a helmsman, too intent
on a lunatic compass ever to feel
his fingers broken by the snarling wheel;
over whose head the waters went
and the whip-thongs of torn sail.
Night fell, and the mast
splintering, passed
pennoned into the jaws of the gale.

Flamboyant signals of distress
erupted from his hand : but dark rain blocked
the golden rain, and tongues of lightning mocked
each muzzled rocket. Rudderless
through all the angles of the chart

his vessel drifted,
till an iron wave lifted
and falling, cracked its timber heart.

There was a castaway, who shook
a captain's coat in the wind's teeth, gave
his buckle-shoes to the pull of the wave;
who risen out of the wreck—
see!—naked as a dolphin swims
into the humbling,
surf-white, tumbling,
sanctuary-harbour of your limbs.

Letter to a Friend

You blame me that I do not write
with the accent of the age :
the eunuch voice of scholarship,
or the reformer's rage
(blurred by a fag-end in the twisted lip).
You blame me that I do not call
truculent nations to unite.
I answer that my poems all
are woven out of love's loose ends;
for myself and for my friends.

You blame me that I do not face
the banner-headline fact
of rape and death in bungalows,
cities and workmen sacked.
Tomorrow's time enough to rant of those,
when the whirlpool sucks us in.
Turn away from the bitter farce,
or have you now forgotten
that cloud, star, leaf, and water's dance
are facts of life, and worth your glance?

You blame me that I do not look
at cities, swivelled, from
the eye of the crazy gunman, or
the man who drops the bomb.
Twenty years watching from an ivory tower,
taller than your chimney-stack,
I have seen fields beyond the smoke :
and think it better that I make
in the sloganed wall the people pass,
a window—not a looking-glass.

Poem upon the Quincentenary of Magdalen College

THE chapel silent and the candles weeping.
White boys erect, each with the sun
alive beneath his skin and gold blood leaping,
stooped in one hour; were levelled soon
with the arterial weeping of despair
into old men. Although a lifetime slips
through this night's sorrow, none will shift his stare.
Their beards shake white below the fluttering lips,
their hands still tremble in the stress of prayer.

They weep because no guests will mourn with them
the dying of five hundred Junes.
Tongued bells are dumb : the requiem
sleeps in the organ's throat, and tunes
swirl only on the tented lawn. No psalms
are scrolled in smoke above the shadow pall,
but for this night, freed from a mason's charms,
the stone musicians tip-toe from the wall
with tabret, lute, and viol in their arms.

For one not lit with eyes the pipers blow
nothing but silver, fiddlers weave
a tent of scarlet with the shuttle bow.
What more should he believe
beyond the kiss of taffeta and shower
of heels? Like shells that toll for their bell-tongued seas
his ears ring back the changes of the hour.
He only understands the prophecies
of iron pigeons gathering in the tower.

It seemed he whistled as the night was failing
a dirge for unremembered years,
and on his face the moth-winged rain was falling
persistent as the candles' tears;
and neither priest nor prophet turned his head
for whirling girls or laughter from the crowd.
These saw the Great Tower gilded : they instead,
through the sarcophagus, through mask and shroud,
saw naked the dimensions of the dead.

Now morning shovels in the sunlight, bringing
a blackbird in the last tail-coat
to raise the requiem. He stills us, singing
in the small chantry of his throat
the song the blind boy whistled through the rain.
The dancers all have dwindled into stone,
the mourners given up their ghosts of flame.
Tabret and lute and kettle-drum alone
in carven hands upon the arch remain.

A Dog's Death

This dying of the dog, now gone to earth
in some abandoned catacomb of the mole,
confronts us with our shadows. In that hole
lies a boy, dead, and crouching by this hearth
a man's dark image. Always I can feel
his hand on mine. We loved the dog, but banish
its name, its basket, and the painted dish,
to shake the clinging shadow from our heel.

As on so many evenings when we set
the last of the china zodiac on its shelf,
the dog would bustle to the door and bark;
in this hushed kitchen I cannot forget
how, at the dropping latch, I would myself
enter the moonblaze or the howling dark.

Epstein's Lazarus

For my father who commissioned this poem

HIS mother's agony at his making—
when he was wrested from the womb—
was not so great. God's son is breaking
the innermost sanctuary of the tomb.
His eyes are twisted to the altar,
the chancel where he cannot hide;
the hand that drags him cannot falter
and his own are bandaged to his side.

Before the stone rolls back, and he is wrenched
into the tall light, stranger on this spot,
pity the mother's son that has been shown
the penalty of love: pity the blenched
face and the anguished eye. If you cannot,
you more than Lazarus are made of stone.

Still Life

A FEATURE of the guest-house window
like the cracked pane and the shrivelled fly,
she drops no stitches if the lap-dogs bark
nor flinches when a bus throbs by.
She who is nobody's wife or widow
sits, like a furled umbrella from the hall,
watching the boys play cricket in the park
and powerless to retrieve their ball.

With a knitting-needle quill all day
she writes the latest chapter of her life
for grandchildren, not hers, to stretch and pull,
rough-handle till it fray. They would not laugh
at the loose hand so readily, if they
could read the breaking heart between the lines.
Pity and terror fit her parable
for the grey language of the skeins.

She does not, like the house-maid, hear the clock
have hourly palpitations on the wall.
She does not hear the chauffeur's double knock
and the jolt of the chest in the hall.
Through the cracked window-pane leaks in the dark
until it seems she scarcely breathes at all;
watching the boys play cricket in the park
and powerless to retrieve their ball.

Sword Dancers

WHILE wind-ropes tugging in the chimney rocked
carillons of stars on Christmas Eve,
we listened for the whispers, and the crunch
of shoes on gravel. No one ever knocked
before the carol. They came in—with laughter
like plumed smoke—crowding to receive
their mince-pie and a glass of punch,
and play the hand-bells after.

Then five boys dancing in a circle shook
the timbers of the hall, until it seemed
that five became five thousand, and ten feet
fell with ten thousand's thunder. At the shock
Troy crashed, and Jericho's rampart tumbled in.
A pattern of swords in the firelight gleamed,
and the fire was a Roman street
and Moscow and Berlin.

From east and west the earthquake armies tramped
westward and eastward, darkening the downs
and steppes and deserts, till horizons rocked
under a red sky. But the marchers stamped
to a halt; bayonet and pike and scimitar
glittered no longer with the blaze of towns;
and the whirling swords were lifted and locked
in one five-pointed star.

The Big Top

Lightning was it, like an axe,
sheared the pole and felled the tent;
or did the yokel-fisted wind
pummel the canvas till it rent;
or was it nothing but the rain
along the ropes collapsed this firmament?

With the Big Top the sky fell down
on the acrobat and clown
and all about one field was hurled
the enormous ruin of the world.

At first light from the caravans
had swaggered trainers with their whips,
and waved them to the swarming men
who carried nails between their lips.
No one who saw the tent go up
had premonition of Apocalypse.

With the Big Top the sky fell down
on the acrobat and clown
and all about one field was hurled
the enormous ruin of the world.

The fattest woman in the world
died of shock. The dwarf crawled out
but would not let them touch his leg,
and wept to hear the jugglers shout
and curse their hands. The circus master
lay quite still in his most scarlet coat.

With the Big Top the sky fell down
on the acrobat and clown
and all about one field was hurled
the enormous ruin of the world.

Not two by two the animals
descended as from Noah's ark.
The high mast killed the elephant;
canvas billows drowned the bark
of sealion and the dancing dogs,
and the tiger mauled the tigress in the dark.

With the Big Top the sky fell down
on the acrobat and clown
and all about one field was hurled
the enormous ruin of the world.

The aquarium was broken; glass
rained over the sawdust floor.
Rainbows died in the tropical fish
and a lamp fell in the ponies' straw.
An audience of clapping flames
eclipsed in a moment the lions' roar.

With the Big Top the sky fell down
on the acrobat and clown
and all about one field was hurled
the enormous ruin of the world.

The Strong Man was pinned down and burnt;
no rescuer saw the canvas surge
before the fire discovered him.
At the crowd's dumbfounded verge
nobody laughed; no children's hands
volleyed to see the chalk-faced clown emerge.

With the Big Top the sky fell down
on the acrobat and clown
and all about one field was hurled
the enormous ruin of the world.

View from an Attic

UNDER the crazy gables of a falling house,
too proud to fall
from chimney-pots and stars
into the common street,
I wait, as the cat waits for his grey mouse.
Shoulder to shoulder stand
books nodding round the wall,
and the pen in my slack hand
sleeps: for no poem in the wainscot stirs
its rhyming feet.

Mind and arena have been cleared, this ambush planned,
since delicate bells
knocked on my window-pane;
and, gloved in silence, brought
the sun on a burning salver to my hand.
On paper never scarred
with ink no stroke foretells
the coming struggle. Hard
must be the hunt before my clawing pen
fastens on thought.

Under the gables until midnight no mouse stirs:
but down, down, down
in the stunned street, I hear
continually the mutter
of engines straddled by the leather riders.
In storm-dark livery
they come. They split the town
with lightning; and I see
beneath the flash burn terrible and clear
the rat in the gutter.

Lament

BECAUSE I have no time
to set my ladder up, and climb
out of the dung and straw,
green poems laid in a dark store
shrivel and grow soft
like unturned apples in a loft.

Shall these Bones Live?

IF all the clocks rang their last chime,
and all the clock-towers toppled, and time
ran down today,
Chaucer and Blake's haphazard bones
would not lift their Abbey stones
and stalk away,
arm in arm, to see the sun
burn out, or the moon's skeleton
wasting and frail as they.

Dying, they put the body down
once and for all like an old gown
in its wooden room.
Each has climbed to a worthier nook
between the white walls of a book
till the knock of doom.
This secret every poet knows :
his nib must cut with chisel-blows
the lettering of his tomb.

Scribo Ergo Sum

The page stares through me, like a mirror
with nothing in its eye
but ceiling or blank sky.

No trick of the light, no paper error
defines this emptiness.
Now I am featureless,

un-selved, without substance or image—
till pen stroke by pen stroke
out of the stubborn block

of the page, forehead and mouth emerge,
mouth moving and moving arm :
I write, therefore I am.

Out of Bounds

THE world was flat, lawn without end,
when first we left the house. Later we stood
at the world's edge over a newfound land
dizzy with orchards. These and the tall wood
contained us for six summers; meadow and
wilderness a seventh. Then we found
the fence that proved the world was round.

We broke out over the dead
limb of a larch and in the Colonel's park
trespassed till supper, trespassed all that year.
Emerging once from the wood's cathedral dark
we saw miles off, but every sail-rib clear,
a windmill standing at ease, its head
laurelled with small, bright clouds. We said,

'We could do it in half a day.'
The sun was in mid flight. Down the first hill
bracken stampeded with us, cantered up
the second, ambled up the third. The mill
like a schooner from wave top to wave top
whenever we closed seemed to veer away:
nautical miles between us lay.

Minute by minute the sun burned
down like a rick into red ash, fading
to grey, then charcoal. We were gaining now
on a giant in seven-league boots, wading
thigh-deep, head-down, over seas of plough
and plunging grass, who as we looked lurched, turned
back; and the darkness churned.

Like skeletal arms the black
sweeps gestured to the sky. One field to cross;
another to go round; a stile; we went
stumbling between tall hedges, and there was
one field more. As if by common consent,
with hardly a word spoken, we turned back
shoulder to shoulder down the track.

Afterwards we said, 'Another time
we will start earlier', but though we went
many fields further, north, south, east and west
of the windmill, by that same consent
we left it undisturbed. Though I have crossed
mountains and seas since, I have yet to climb
a hill not seven miles from home.

To climb for what? To find a grey
skull, lichened, cobweb-raftered, with the wind
a ghost lamenting through its broken teeth?
Better to leave the features undefined
than rob the landscape of a last wild myth.
Still the sweeps signal in my head: are they
beckoning, or waving us away?

First Blood

It was. The breech smelling of oil,
the stock of resin—buried snug
in the shoulder. Not too much recoil
at the firing of the first slug

(jubilantly into the air)
nor yet too little. Targets pinned
against a tree : shot down : and there
abandoned to the sniping wind.

My turn first to carry the gun.
Indian file and camouflaged
with contours of green shade and sun
we ghosted between larch and larch.

A movement between branches—thump
of a fallen cone. The barrel
jumps, making branches jump
higher, dislodging the squirrel

to the next tree. Your turn, my turn.
The silhouette retracts its head.
A hit. 'Let's go back to the lawn.'
'We can't leave it carrying lead

for the rest of its life. Reload.
Finish him off. Reload again.'
It was now *him*, and when he showed
the sky cracked like a window pane.

He broke away : traversed a full
half dozen trees : vanished. Had found
a hole? We watched that terrible
slow spiral to the clubbing ground.

His back was to the tree. His eyes
were gun barrels. He was dumb,
and we could not see past the size
of his hands or hear for the drum

in his side. Four shots point-blank
to dull his eyes, a fifth to stop
the shiver in his clotted flank.
A fling of earth. As we stood up

the larches closed their ranks. And when
earth would not muffle the drumming blood
we, like dishonoured soldiers, ran
the gauntlet of a darkening wood.

Miss Lavender

Miss Lavender taught us to ride
clamping halfcrowns between saddle and knee
on Sunday afternoons
in a watermeadow one mile wide :
and the hot halfcrowns
she would keep, after an hour, for her fee.

Her horses stepped like a king's own
always to imperatives of Spanish drill.
Miss Lavender said,
'A horseman has to be thrown
ten times.' From thoroughbred
to exploding grass we headoverheeled; until

that March the watermeadow froze
and Miss Lavender died, consumptive
on a stable floor
among motionless horses. Those
died after for no reason, or
for want of a Spanish imperative.

No Ordinary Sunday

No ordinary Sunday. First the light
falling dead through dormitory windows blind
with fog; and then, at breakfast, every plate
stained with the small, red cotton flower; and no
sixpence for pocketmoney. Greatcoats, lined
by the right, marched from their pegs, with slow
poppy fires smouldering in one lapel
to light us through the fallen cloud. Behind
that handkerchief sobbed the quick Sunday bell.

A granite cross, the school field underfoot,
inaudible prayers, hymn-sheets that stirred
too loudly in the hand. When hymns ran out,
silence, like silt, lay round so wide and deep
it seemed that winter held its breath. We heard
only the river talking in its sleep :
until the bugler flexed his lips, and sound
cutting the fog cleanly like a bird,
circled and sang out over the bandaged ground.

Then, low voiced, the headmaster called the roll
of those who could not answer; every name
suffixed with honour—'double first', 'kept goal
for Cambridge'—and a death—in spitfires, tanks,
and ships torpedoed. At his call there came
through the mist blond heroes in broad ranks
with rainbows struggling on their chests. Ahead
of us, in strict step, as we idled home
marched the formations of the towering dead.

November again, and the bugles blown
in a tropical Holy Trinity,
the heroes today stand further off, grown

smaller but distinct. They flash no medals, keep
no ranks : through *Last Post* and *Reveille*
their chins loll on their chests, like birds asleep.
Only when the long, last note ascends
upon the wings of kites, some two or three
look up : and have the faces of my friends.

War Story

of one who grew up at Gallipoli
not over months and miles, but in the space
of feet and half a minute. Wading shoreward
with a plague of bullets pocking the sea
he tripped, as it seemed to him over his scabbard,
and stubbed his fingers on a dead man's face.

Traveller's Choice

COUNSEL yourself that traveller
who in a fiery desert found,
when half starved for water,
a well-shaft glimmering in the ground—
no rope nor bucket to be had
and the sweet water twenty foot down—
should he crouch in the heat and go mad
or plunge into coolness and drown?

After an Amputation

AFTER an amputation, he had heard,
the patient feels his missing limb
foreshortened, still a part of him
but like a snail's horn shrinking; and his hurt
more of the truncheon than the knife.
The surgeons did their work. Through life
the ache persisted, somewhere between heart
and head. His boyhood every day
crept closer as he moved away.

The Legacy

My sons, if there should be
those to accept from me
my father's legacy,
will find there must be met
not only the old debt,
but that of wounds still wet.

Letter to my Sisters

ASLEEP till nine, again you break
your croissants by the tideless lake
where small fish quarrel for crumbs
and, making with its paddle-beat
no more stir than a swan's feet,
the day's first steamer comes

obliquely to the landing stage.
At ten you walk into the village
for the long hot loaves and cheese
to be eaten as you lie
halfway to a Renaissance sky
among the crocuses and bees.

As my days have been, your day is.
Cowbells and churchbell and the kiss
of scythes in tilting pastures shake
the web of silence, but your look
seldom travels from your book.
The sun takes a turn round the lake.

Only when evening throws the last
steamer like a dart burning past
the point, and ghostly waiters
whisper that supper is soon,
will you stumble down as the moon
stumbles on the tideless waters.

The moon is a periscope in which
an exile like myself may watch,
over mountains rough as broken glass,
others who prepare to make
their longest journey from the lake
into the formidable pass.

All see only the green incline.
So many have crossed that skyline
singing, and none of them come back
to tell how night in the ravine
cut them off like a guillotine,
still there is singing on the track.

Darkness and mist and the false echo
divide the singers, and snow
cancels each step. Some as they clamber
lonely over glaciers find,
imprisoned under ice, a friend
like an insect in green amber.

But here the sun, in rising, makes
bonfires of the embattled peaks.
Winds have sung with us; and we
in exultation have seen,
distant but luminous between
mountain and mountain, the tidal sea.

Little sisters, about to climb
beyond your valley for the first time,
what can I give you—talisman
or map—that may guide you straight
into a plain as temperate
as the valley where we began?

Not my example, certainly.
Only my love—and this: I see,
whenever the going is rough,
those who defy foul weather
and avalanche are roped together
and the rope is love.

From W. B. Yeats to his friend Maud Gonne

From W. B. Yeats to his friend Maud Gonne.
The writing modest as the words upon
the title-page. Him I can understand;
picture him turning the pen in his hand
considering what to write: something not cold
nor yet embarrassingly overbold.
But in the gallery where my portraits are
I cannot see the heart that, set ajar
for anarchists and peasants and sick birds,
could not be crowbarred open by such words
as break the heart of time; that fountained out
in tears or laughter at a newsboy's shout—
only to the poet remaining shut
as these clenched pages that she never cut.

Death of a Clown

THAT melancholy man the clown
before the mirror in his tent
lowered like any king his crown
the ginger wig upon his head,
attached a rubber nose, and went
down the dark passage when the light winked red.

Act five, scene one.
The gangway lights go down :
the band strikes up. 'He's on—
Homo the clown !'

Out of his tunnel, as a bull
rosetted for the ring explodes
into the light that pricks its skull,
he gallops into the desert. Sand
tackles his ankles (which forebodes
burial, like the slow pulse of the band).

Act five, scene two.
Dazed by so dense a stare
he turns, uncertain who
to charge, or where.

Spot-light suns in a canvas sky
have marked him for their own. He stands
balancing beams fifty foot high
of hot gold on his head. The dark
lures and eludes him. His two hands
manipulate oranges into an arc.

Act five, scene three.
The band quicken their beat,
following *Colonel Bogey*
with the *Firebird Suite*.

A parody of Shadrach
entering the fiery furnace,
he turns a front-somersault, back-
somersault, head over heels through
twelve hoops of flame; while in his face
rouge roses glister with a bloody dew.

Act five, scene four.
From that ordeal by fire
to this by air : the awe-
compelling wire.

Inching like Icarus under
the sun and over that far sphere
of sand, heel and toe blunder.
Umbrella wings, turned inside out,
whack once the air. Some see, all hear
the soft body falling like a pheasant shot.

Act five, scene five.
Clumsily, at the run
the stretcher-men arrive,
and the show goes on

as he goes off, along the long
tunnel before the last. The band,
far off, are blowing and bowing wrong
notes thick as flies; nobody claps,
as from disharmony and sand
to air and harmony Icarus escapes.

Toulouse Lautrec at the Moulin Rouge

'Cognac—more cognac for Monsieur Lautrec—
more cognac for the little gentleman,
monster or clown of the Moulin—quick—
his glass is falling! more!'
                                        The Can-Can
chorus with their jet net stockings
and their red heads rocking
have brought the patrons flocking to the floor—
pince-nez, glancing down from legs advancing
to five fingers dancing
over a menu-card, scorn and adore
prostitutes and skinny flirts
who crossing arms and tossing skirts
high-kick—a quick
eye captures all before they fall—
quick lines, thick lines
trace the huge ache under rouge.

'Cognac—more cognac!' Only the slop
of a charwoman pushing her bucket and mop,
and the rattle of chairs on a table top.
The glass can fall no further. Time to stop
the charcoal's passionate waltzing with the hand.
Time to take up the hat, drag out the sticks,
and very slowly, like a hurt crab, stand:
with one wry bow to the vanished band,
launch out with short steps harder than high kicks
along the unspeakable inches of the street.
His flesh was his misfortune: but the feet
of those whose flesh was all their fortune, beat
softly as the grey rain falling
through his brain recalling
Marie, Annette, Jean-Claude, and Marguerite.

The Assault

As the mad woman cried out in the square,
when every hand was hauling on a rope
or levering gates from hinges there—
gates never forced in ten years' war :
'A rape is avenged, avenged with a rape !'

Because, being mad, she could not comprehend
the soldiers' back-slapping and the women's joy,
they did not stop her mouth or send
her packing as they strained
to manoeuvre the stallion into Troy.

The foreign god was of such size, the gate
so stiff, so narrow the ways of the town,
that though the heroes pulled their weight
and the crowd levered, it was late
before they threw their ropes and levers down.

As for a carnival or wedding rite
from every bracket in every room
pine torches fountained their scented light.
There had not been such a lovers' night
not since Paris brought that Helen home.

Embraced and garlanded, the soldiers all
with a girl on one arm instead of a shield
danced round the horse and round the wall
swallowing wine by the helmet full;
then two by two into the darkness reeled.

Only the mad woman huddled alone
in a doorway after, saw shadows fall
from horse's belly to pavement stone
and scatter, scatter, like leaves blown
into a shadow drift under the wall.

As the swan, as Paris, so now the horse
in the dark of the city dropped his seed.
Now life and death must run their course.
Foundations riven by that force
recoil already and the housetops bleed.

Mad woman, mad woman, mad woman—no—
feeling the city shudder, hearing it moan—
not mad enough—better to go
mad as the moon herself than know
the city's end an image of my own.

The Trap

The first night that the monster lurched
out of the forest on all fours,
he saw its shadow in his dream
circle the house, as though it searched
for one it loved or hated. Claws
on gravel and a rabbit's scream
ripped the fabric of his dream.

Waking between dark and dawn
and sodden sheets, his reason quelled
the shadow and the nightmare sound.
The second night it crossed the lawn
a brute voice in the darkness yelled.
He struggled up, woke raving, found
his wall-flowers trampled to the ground.

When rook wings beckoned the shadows back
he took his rifle down, and stood
all night against the leaded glass.
The moon ticked round. He saw the black
elm-skeletons in the doomsday wood,
the sailing and the failing stars
and red coals dropping between bars.

The third night such a putrid breath
fouled, flared his nostrils, that he turned,
turned, but could not lift, his head.
A coverlet as thick as death
oppressed him; he crawled out; discerned
across the door his watchdog, dead.
'Build a trap', the neighbours said.

All that day he built his trap
with metal jaws and a spring as thick
as the neck of a man. One touch
triggered the hanging teeth : jump, snap,
and lightning guillotined the stick
thrust in its throat. With gun and torch
he set his engine in the porch.

The fourth night in their beds appalled
his neighbours heard the hunting roar
mount, mount to an exultant shriek.
At daybreak timidly they called
his name, climbed through the splintered door,
and found him sprawling in the wreck,
naked, with a severed neck.

The Last Mystery

He knew that coastline—no man better—
knew all its rocks and currents, like the veins
and knuckles on the brown back of his hand;
the leap-frog rollers and tall tons that batter
boat-rib and man-rib into grains
of indistinguishable sand:
he had know them all since he could stand.

A shanty was his earliest lullaby,
the beach his back-yard, flotsam all his toys.
He was admitted to the mystery
of tides; read the wind's writing on the sky;
could out-sail, out-dive, out-swim boys
older by half; was known to save
many from the sabre-toothed, man-eating wave.

Knowing so well the temper of that coast,
and all subaqueous hazards of the sea,
what voice, thought, impulse lugged him from his ale
(when every flag was fighting with a mast
and waves kicked bollards off the quay)
to match his Lilliputian sail
against the wrestling muscles of the gale?

Only the lemming knows; his friends knew only
boat-rib and man-rib littered the long shore
many tides after. I declare he fell
like a pearl-dazzled diver through the sea
to that last mystery on its floor:
whose is the heart-beat under the swell,
the hand that turns the whirlpool and the shell?

Closed Circuit

THE fan revolving overhead
afflicts him supine on his bed;
the fan revolving, and a fly
in the closed circuit of one eye
revolving without stop or sound.
Fan and fly drive one thought round
the mind's well like a blindfold horse:
that he is bound on the same course,
revolving blindfold in the grooves
his own blunt feet have made. Thought-hooves
thud on, the roller turns, the rope
returning tilts the bucket up
as empty as it travelled down.
No water there to drink or drown
in, cup of centrifugal force
to fling him like a star off course
into who knows what new dimension.
The clock solicits his attention
to the plain facts of his case.
One finger wagging in his face
(and, oh, meticulous consonants!)
stress, lawyer-like, the relevance
of Time. Somewhere a gramophone
under the needle starts to moan
as a man delirious. Fan, fly,
clock, record drill into eye
and ear. He jumps up, looks up, sees
outside, like autumn vortices,
only and everywhere the brown
kites spiralling above the town.

Sindhi Woman

Barefoot through the bazaar,
and with the same undulant grace
as the cloth blown back from her face,
she glides with a stone jar
high on her head
and not a ripple in her tread.

Watching her cross erect
stones, garbage, excrement, and crumbs
of glass in the Karachi slums,
I, with my stoop, reflect
they stand most straight
who learn to walk beneath a weight.

Camel

Though come down in the world to pulling a cart
piled high as a house-top, camel, your gait
proclaims, proclaims, proclaims the aristocrat.

Though your knees, like a clown's, wear bells that clash
whenever your cushion-feet cuff the street,
a greater clown behind you swings the lash

over your backside. History and he
are unacquainted. From your ancestors
you have inherited history;

philosophy becomes you like your hump;
nobility speaks louder than these sores
and bells and the sweat on your angular rump.

I have seen your nostrils flare to a wind
born nowhere in the port or festering slums,
but in the wastes beyond the wastes of Sind.

Heavily falls the lash. You neither turn
nor flinch, but hooded in your eye there comes
a glint of snows above Baluchistan.

In the Street of the Fruit Stalls

WICKS balance flame, a dark dew falls
in the street of the fruit stalls.
Melon, guava, mandarin,
pyramid-piled like cannon balls,
glow red-hot, gold-hot, from within.

Dark children with a coin to spend
enter the lantern's orbit; find
melon, guava, mandarin—
the moon compacted to a rind,
the sun in a pitted skin.

They take it, break it open, let
a gold or silver fountain wet
mouth, fingers, cheek, nose, chin :
radiant as lanterns they forget
the dark street I am standing in.

The Face

ON the wall above the basins in the barber's shop
a bland face, shaven like a full moon,
salutes the lathered citizen when he looks up.

In the cinema foyer, café and saloon,
at the orphan's shoulder and the widow's side,
floats a face convivial as a child's balloon.

Day after day, milk-churn teeth in a mouth as wide
as a newspaper column or a newsreel screen
welcome an ambassador, dazzle a girl-guide.

Blessed and benevolent full-face! But profile seen
framed in the window of a car, perhaps,
(unflagged and without escort, arrowing between

office and home), the contours of the mask collapse
and tighten. Fat smiles starve as thin as glass;
only to trespass on the frontier of the lips

should tyres, like tongues, spit on you as they pass.

First of the Migrants

First of the migrants, overnight they say
Naz flew to London. She will glide no more
vivid as a rainbow through this door
with her sketch-book under an arm. Today,
missing her small step, one imagines
the rainbow sari in a Georgian square
painting the wind; bus-queues turning to stare
at a bird of Paradise among pigeons.

Last Post

THE Garden Member with the walking stick
grasped like a baton in his British hand
deploys his seeds against the spring attack.
Here thin red line and hollow square stand
stiff in his eye already : wind shot
and the sun's crossfire rake them but break them not.

He sites a trench, waves up more gardeners
to dig the front line in—'This privet hedge
will give them cover but wants cutting'. Shears
scissor behind him. Idler on the edge
of the battlefield, lolled in a wicker chair,
I lay my book down, sniff the smokeless air,

and reflect that evening best becomes
the Imperial-Barrack style. Bearers now throw
tall shutters open on to empty rooms,
as men besieged prop corpses in a row,
gunner by rifleman each at his post
drawing the sniper's fire. Almost

I am deceived. Time, liquid now as light,
drains from the roofs and like a school of whales
the Club buildings surface into night.
Behind these windows and behind these walls
field-officers are pulling on their boots
and monkey-jackets, lighting up cheroots.

Rowels chime on the stair. Glasses chime after
down colonnades where civil servants talk
of civil servants and a fist of laughter
thumps the air. Some, shadow by shadow, walk
about the garden. At their coming, palms
like supplicants make their salaams.

Kites crowd in the peepul tree. The sun,
ripest of windfalls, plummets to the ground.
Time passes. Dinner gong like evening gun
recalls the Garden Member, and its sound
recalls my ghosts to their element. I
go in. From the top of the stairs the sky

has doubled its girth, the garden decreased
to a moat. The eye swims over and sees
ghost-minarets and shadow gables. East
and west of my window two embassies
island the dark with light—our Scylla
and Charybdis, Russia, America.

Around them and beyond them like camp fires burn
the town and harbour galaxies. Tonight,
how many sahibs, whiskey-fisted, turn
to the garden wall that bounds their sight;
sensing, uneasily, in the street
a menace abroad they cannot meet

with crossed Lee Enfields from the library wall?
Not many now: most are laid underground,
but armchairs like Titan bones lumber the hall,
humbling us. We are hushed by the sound
of their silence. Light but no voices come
out of their hundred windows. Watching them,

I am reminded of Heorot, home
of the good Hrothgar, in that season
when his bachelors' mouths were stuffed with loam
instead of boasts, laughter or venison—
Heorot with its high seat empty in the hall
and Grendel's shadow growing on the wall.

The Swimming Pool

THE swimming pool by night in summer
lying floodlit, grape-green, from below,
holds up to us in its long mirror
beauty and indolence; but now—
struck by the lash of a late swimmer—

writhes with a hundred hands. This tender moon
bares knuckles, coolie knuckles, taut
as wire on pick and spade, in May's noon
furnace digging for the sport
of manicured hands in the monsoon.

The swimmer, turning with an otter swirl
in the deep end, revives the quick
convulsion of a sun-struck fool
of a navvy who broke his neck;
but that was soon smoothed over, as now the pool.

Tent-Pegging at Night

THE four greys fidget as a torch-boy runs
down wind across the *maidan* lighting pegs.
Spurred now by trumpets they take off like swans
with steady necks above a blur of legs.

Headlong horsemen, when the flames blow back,
see them as flags over Panipat plain.
Louder than hooves and trumpets they invoke
the Most High God. Moghuls again

lean from the saddle. Beside the stirrup
their level lances stoop towards the mark—
stoop lower—kick—and catherinewheeling up
proffer their flames to the devouring dark.

'Here comes Sir George'

THE boys wink at the boys: 'Here comes Sir George.'
Yes, here he comes, punctual as nine o'clock
with bad jokes buzzing at his ramrod back—
'Victoria's Uncle', 'Rearguard of the Raj'.

They do not know or, if they know, forget
the old fool held a province down larger
than England; not as a Maharaja
prodigal with silver and bayonet;

but with cool sense, authority and charm
that still attend him, crossing a room
with the *Odes of Horace* under his arm
and in his button-hole a fresh-cut bloom.

Honour the rearguard, you half-men, for it
was, in retreat, the post of honour. He—
last of the titans—is worth your study.
You are not worth the unsheathing of his wit.

The Peshawar Vale Hunt

THE Peshawar Vale Hunt has gone to ground.
Over its earth foxes laugh
last, for the loud-mouthed master, horn and hound
are at a loss for sound.

In the Horsehoe Bar of the Club with half
an hour to kill, I raise my drink
in mock salute to a damp-mottled, buff
Hunt Breakfast photograph

of nineteen-ten. In coats of Kipling-pink,
the colour of their map, the bloody
subalterns and iron maidens link
arms, leer, try not to blink

before the camera blinks. If they could see
themselves now, grouped on the grass
in their insolent poses! History
has put down the mighty

from their family seats; tumbled them, arse
over crop, out of the saddle.
The poor inherit the earth; the middle class
take care of the brass.

You, with your hair parted down the middle,
officer, gentleman and all
that, today you are sentenced by little
brown men of less rare metal.

Empire Builder, with your back to the wall,
have you any last word to say?
'It is better to ride fiercely, and fall,
than never to ride at all.'

Cowboys

panther-footed saunter in the street,
who spinning six blunt sounds in the mouth's chamber
tongue-hammer them one by one when they meet.

Evening. Eyes sharpen under sombre
brims, drilling the distance for a spurt of hooves.
These wait only for the Stage to lumber

between sights, to squander their nine lives
(in a town now dead from the waist up,
for where are the children and the shopping wives?)

They saunter with slack hands, but at the drop
of a card will conjure guns out of thick air—
explode every bottle on the bar-top—

eclipse the lamp with a shooting star—
struggle under tables, until the one
with the grin knock senseless the one with the scar.

Justice done and seen to be done,
a bullet in front for one in the back,
the honest stranger on the white stallion

canters off singing. Shopkeeper and clerk
lunge to their panther feet in the one-and-nines,
saunter slack-handed into the dark,

and manfully ride home their bucking trains:
each wearing, like a medal, his chosen wound
to cancel the reproach of varicose veins.

Bread and Circuses

He went to the cinema; saw
an arena, faces, sand;
in either wall a door
opening, opening, and
in either door a gladiator.

The toga'd emperor he saw stand
conducting his applause
with an outflung hand,
and the gladiators
looking up at him from the sand :

a classic frieze. Then a ring rain-
bowed down and metal struck
metal, flashed, struck again.
Feet circled in a ruck
of sand, scarred with a widening stain.

The candid camera rolled its eye
up to the Roman crowd;
hands hammering the sky,
wolf-throats baying aloud
that one of their own kind should die.

Cheated of action in that pause,
having no interest
in the white of eyes and jaws,
he looked down, half noticed
hands fastened on his knees, like claws.

Quiet Wedding

WAITING so patiently for Mr Right
the six-foot millionaire to carry her off,
she sat indoors and knitted. Every night
she supped and sipped a magazine; until
sitting too long by windows brought a cough;
the cough—too long neglected—brought a chill;
the chill brought on pneumonia. Her light
at lunchtime brought the caretaker. She died
with cases packed, her passport up to date.
Black car, white flowers arrived : a nephew cried
at the reception. From that afternoon
she smiled. Retiring early she slept late
fulfilling all her dreams of honeymoon,
virgin forever and forever bride.

Witch's Sacrament

'Ritual' is perhaps too large a word:
but every night the small-boned lady,
like a faggot of firewood, makes her eddy
against the solid men flooding homeward
over the bombsite to the Underground.
Her back to the dark tide, crouching, she unwraps
fish-heads (with paper eyes) and liver scraps.
Her familiars rise to meet her with no sound.

Through the fence's broken teeth they take
the witch's sacrament, and their eyes connect
with a flight of sparks, which suddenly break
formation and burn out. Returning under
the earth her step is supple, her eyes reflect
a bonfire flowering from the breast's tinder.

Encounter

'They told me you would come alone
and peaceably to my side,
but there are armed men at your back.'
Said the bridegroom to the bride.
'Tall and white as a candle
of incandescent wax
your body lights up rifle,
bayonet and battle-axe.'
'Armed men are standing at your own.'
The lady to her love replied.

'History has signed them with its scars,
signed metal at each man's side,
but what have they to do with us?'
Said the bridegroom to the bride.
'I only know they look as men
whose ammunition ends
in some beleaguered garrison,
and ask if death or friends
confront them in the narrow pass.'
The lady to her love replied.

'Why do no trumpeter's alarms
deafen the mountain side,
no drums from two such armies sound?'
Said the bridegroom to the bride.
'Two armies, but their single shout
flung up and rolling round,
see here! has blown our candle out.
I tremble as the ground
trembles beneath their falling arms.'
The lady to her love replied.

Feet off the Ground

ON the ground floor the wealthy and their cats
minded each other's business, but above
in the topmost branches of the flats
two, like their neighbours, lived on crusts and love.

Sparrow jazz shook them awake; pigeon hymns,
sacred on Sunday, all the week profane,
composed at nightfall their haphazard limbs.
And a crow made its pulpit in the drain.

If sometimes, towards evening, he let fall
out of his fingers' nest a clutch of words,
singing poured out of the window, and all
her birds were poems and all his poems birds.

Green Thought

I do not know much about love, but I know
it is common as grass which, although
it refuse at times to take root on a lawn,
can bury a bombsite, split asphalt, and grow
in any ditch, niche, or gutter where winds blow
or sparrow-boys brawl. This much I learn
from an old man who has limped up the path
to warm his feet, and more than his feet, at our hearth.

His scrupulous tweeds and courtesy
have taken their place at the ritual tea
on Sunday afternoons; a ritual
for him, whose shrine this is, especially.
A girl, not yet his wife, runs for more tea
into the singing kitchen. From the hall
her footsteps chatter, and soon her face
will laugh in the mirror over the mantelpiece.

He is watching—over his cup between
fireplace and door—a princess not nineteen.
We too remember her, though she appears
to us as the tall, gaunt, tragedy-queen
whom illness kept indoors, who dressed in green
throughout all seasons. We remember tears;
agonies the doctors could not understand;
tantrums, and the last tantrum ended by her hand.

But most the legend of her funeral
dominates memory: how there fell,

miraculous as manna, a swift wing
of snow, not heavily like a pall
but thin as moonlight. It transfigured all
mourners to alabaster, cancelling
veils, toecaps, collars, cancelling the sound
of the white coffin lowered into the white ground.

Today as he talks, smiles, drinks his tea,
smiles, talks of earlier Sundays, I can see
one picture only : him, brought to the brink
of the grave, and the grave suddenly
healed with fine snow, and every tree
in sight bowing a moonlit head. I think
love is like that : merciful as snow
bandaging the bruised earth, white making the green grow.